Table of Contents

SALADS

BREADS

SOUPS

MAINS

SIDES

QUICK & EASY
GERMAN RECIPES

The Budget German Kitchen

AMAZING EVERYDAY MEALS THAT GO FURTHER

GERHILD FULSON
@justlikeoma

Quick & Easy German Recipes: The Budget German Kitchen

Published by Fulson Web Publishing, 2026

ISBN: 978-1-997886-05-1

Cover and book design by Michael Fulson, simplycreativebranding.com

Photography by Gerhild Fulson

www.fulsonweb.com
www.justlikeoma.com
www.quick-german-recipes.com
www.facebook.com/justlikeoma

DESSERTS

INDEX

Introduction

Some of the best German meals aren't the fancy ones. They're the ones that feed a family, stretch what you have, and still taste like home.

If you grew up with German cooking, you already know what I mean: a pot of soup that somehow made everything feel better, potatoes turned into something comforting and filling, or a simple pan meal of onions, eggs, and whatever was left in the fridge—yet it still tasted like something *Mutti* would proudly put on the table.

When my *mutti* and *papa* immigrated to Canada in the 1950s, *Mutti* had to be creative in the kitchen. Ingredients were different and money was tight, yet she was determined to keep our Germany food traditions alive. And she did. She experimented, adjusted, and made it work, without losing the flavors she loved.

That's the heart of this cookbook.

Because if there's one thing German home cooking does well, it's this: it turns basic ingredients into something warm, satisfying, and truly delicious. You don't need expensive cuts of meat or a pantry full of specialty items. You just need a few good staples, some smart shortcuts, and a little *oma* know-how.

Inside, you'll find budget-friendly German recipes that are simple to make, family-tested, and full of that *"all's right with the world"* comfort. From soups and one-pot meals to hearty sides, easy dinners, and a few sweet treats that can absolutely count as supper, these are the recipes you'll come back to again and again.

So grab your pot, your pan, and your wooden spoon. Let's cook the German way: practical, comforting, and so *lecker*.

Tschüss!

Oma Gerhild❤

Remake the Leftovers

One of the easiest ways to keep German cooking budget-friendly is to cook once, then remake it into something new.

Many of the recipes in this book were born from exactly that idea, using what you already have and turning it into a fresh meal that still feels hearty and homemade.

Potatoes:
Leftover potatoes are especially useful. They can become *Bratkartoffeln* (page 72) or bulk up *Gemüsefrittata* (page 54). Even a simple bowl of mashed potatoes can become tomorrow's side dish with *Senfeier* (page 66), spinach, or cabbage.

Soups:
Soups are another smart place to stretch your groceries. Vegetable soup, lentil soup, carrot soup, and potato cabbage soup all welcome odds and ends from the fridge or freezer. A handful of frozen vegetables, a few extra potatoes, or even a spoonful of instant mashed potato flakes can turn a thin soup into a proper meal.

Chicken:
Rotisserie chicken is also a budget hero. Use some of the meat for Chicken Fricassee (page 56), then turn the rest of the meat and carcass into Chicken Noodle Soup (page 38). That's two meals for four people from one inexpensive chicken, and it tastes like you planned it that way.

Bread:
Don't forget the sweet leftovers. Bread that is past its best becomes *Arme Ritter* (page 50), and extra dough from *strudel* or rolls can be frozen so your next baking day is already half done.

In other words, *if you have leftovers, you have options*. That's doing it *Just Like Oma!*

Budget Boosters

Seasonal Price Tips:

Buy what is cheapest, and you can make the same yummy meals from this cookbook with small swaps. Keeping your grocery bill steady while still cooking the dishes you love is just how *Oma* does it!

Winter:

- Cabbage, potatoes, onions, carrots (soups, cabbage sides, fried potatoes).
- Shelf-stable baking staples (flour, sugar, yeast) often go on sale around Christmas time.

Spring:

- Eggs and dairy are often steady; lean on Frittata (page 54), *Senfeier* (page 66), and soups to keep costs predictable.
- Use frozen vegetables when fresh ones spike in price.

Summer:

- Cucumbers and green beans can be inexpensive in season; use them for *Bohnensalat* (page 12) and *Gurkensalat* (page 14).
- Berries and stone fruit may be cheaper, but apples remain a reliable budget fruit for baking.

Fall:

- Apples usually offer best value; *Himmel und Erde* (page 74) and the apple desserts can be seasonal anchors.
- Cabbage and root vegetables return to peak value; ideal for *Krautsalat* (page 18), Cabbage Soup (page 44), and *Rotkohl* (page 78).

Shopping habits that can lower total meal cost:

- Plan around one anchor sale per week (for example, discounted eggs, potatoes, or cabbage).
- Use frozen vegetables strategically in soups and skillets to reduce waste.
- Buy a larger bag of onions and potatoes if storage space allows.

Budget Boosters

Pantry staples:

See pages 96–97 for the **Pantry Staples** shopping list.

Essentials:

- ○ Potatoes, onions, and apples (the backbone of *Himmel und Erde*, potato sides, and multiple soups)
- ○ Cabbage (for *Krautsalat*, Braised Cabbage, Cabbage Soup, and as a low-cost volume builder)
- ○ Eggs (for *Senfeier*, Frittata, *Bauernfrühstück*, *Arme Ritter*, *Kaiserschmarrn*)
- ○ Flour, baking powder and yeast (for *Brötchen*, *Krustenbrot*, Pretzels, and desserts)
- ○ Mustard and vinegar (quick flavor for salads, *Senfeier* sauce balance, and overall brightness)
- ○ Bouillon or broth base (for *Gemüsesuppe*, Cabbage-Potato Soup, Lentil Soup, and as a low-cost flavor multiplier)
- ○ Neutral oil and butter (for baking plus pan-frying potatoes, pancakes, and cabbage)

Budget Multipliers:

Increase flavor without increasing cost.

- ○ Tomato paste (small amounts deepen soups and hashes)
- ○ Paprika (sweet), nutmeg, cinnamon, bay leaves, black pepper
- ○ Caraway seeds (optional but classic for cabbage and some breads)
- ○ Cornstarch (for thickening sauces and puddings)
- ○ Breadcrumbs or stale bread (for topping bakes and for minimizing waste; also for *Arme Ritter*)
- ○ Rice and lentils (low cost per serving, shelf-stable, and filling)

Common fridge & freezer items that reduce waste:

- ○ Milk or shelf-stable milk; sour cream or plain yogurt (choose one)
- ○ Frozen peas or mixed vegetables (stretch soups and skillet meals)
- ○ Frozen berries (optional, mainly for baking if you include fruit variations)
- ○ One affordable cheese (optional topping for *Bauernfrühstück* or skillet meals)

Recipe-specific staples:

Items to buy if you're using these often.

- ○ CREAM OF WHEAT *(Grieß)* for the roasted CREAM OF WHEAT soup
- ○ Canned beets for beet soup
- ○ Cucumbers and green beans (fresh in season; frozen works well for bean salad)
- ○ Baking soda for Pretzels and Pretzel Rolls

Budget Boosters

Smart Swaps:

High-impact swaps that you can use, sorted by ingredient category.

INGREDIENT OR ITEM	USED IN THIS BOOK	LOW-COST SWAPS	NOTES
Sour cream	Potato Pancakes, Potato & Cabbage Soup	Plain yogurt (same amount)	*Yogurt adds tang and is often cheaper; avoid flavored.*
Milk	Baking, sauces, soups	Shelf-stable milk or powdered milk	*Use what you already buy regularly to reduce waste.*
Butter	Baking, cabbage, potatoes, pancakes	Half butter, half neutral oil in pan-frying	*Do not swap 1:1 in baking unless recipe states.*
Mustard	*Senfeier*, salad dressings, flavor finishing	Any mustard you like; start mild and adjust	*Mustard + vinegar fixes many budget dishes.*
Broth	*Gemüsesuppe*, Lentil Soup, Cabbage-Potato Soup	Bouillon + water	*Keep bouillon as a core staple.*
Corned beef	*Labskaus*, *Reisfleisch*	Canned corned beef, cooked ham, or omit and add more onion and seasoning	*If swapping, keep salt in check.*

INGREDIENT OR ITEM	USED IN THIS BOOK	LOW-COST SWAPS	NOTES
Bacon/ham flavor	Optional in soups and cabbage dishes	Smoked paprika or a small amount of smoked sausage	*Use as a flavor accent, not a main ingredient.*
Fresh green beans	*Bohnensalat*	Frozen green beans	*Blanch and cool before dressing to keep texture.*
Fresh cucumber	*Gurkensalat*	English cucumber or field cucumber; use what is cheapest	*Salt-and-drain step reduces watery salad.*
Apples	*Himmel und Erde*, Carrot-Apple Salad, apple bakes	Softer apples for cooking; any affordable apple works	*Use bruised apples for cooking, save best for eating.*
Flour	Breads and baking	Store-brand all-purpose flour	*For breads, consistent brand helps repeatability.*
Yeast	*Brötchen*, *Krustenbrot*, Pretzels	Buy instant yeast in larger pack if cheaper	*Store extra yeast in freezer for longevity.*
Vegetables in soups	*Gemüsesuppe*, Carrot Soup, Lentil Soup	Frozen mixed vegetables	*Frozen often reduces waste and cost.*
Pancakes/*Flädle*	*Flädlesuppe*	Use leftover pancakes or thin crepes	*Batch cook and freeze; slice when frozen for clean strips.*

Budget Boosters

More About Leftovers & Cross-Recipe Ideas:

Leftovers aren't a problem if you cook with a little planning. When you make a bit extra of the right basics, you can turn them into fresh meals later in the week. That means fewer forgotten containers and fewer expensive midweek grocery runs.

Ingredients that connect multiple recipes:

Breads:

Use *Brötchen* (page 22), Pretzels (page 24), and *Krustenbrot* (page 28) as soup sides, crumbs for toppings, or as the base for *Arme Ritter* (page 50).

Potatoes:

Cook extra once, then reuse for *Bauernfrühstück* (page 52), *Bratkartoffeln* (page 72), and *Schupfnudeln* (page 80).

Cabbage:

One head of cabbage can stretch across three dishes: *Krautsalat* (page 18), *Kohlsuppe mit Kartoffeln* (page 44), and *Weisskraut* (page 70).

Apples:

Use fresh apples for *Karotten-Apfel-Salat* (page 16), and cooked apples for *Himmel und Erde* (page 74) and the apple desserts.

Eggs:

Used in *Bauernfrühstück* (page 52), *Frittata* (page 54), *Senfeier* (page 66), and as an easy protein boost for simple meals.

Pancakes:

Batch-cook *Flädlesuppe* (page 34) and *Kaiserschmarrn* (page 92), then freeze extras for later.

Three quick "remake" formulas:

Soup:
Leftover soup + extra potatoes or rice + frozen vegetables. Taste, then add a small splash of vinegar.

Skillet:
Onions + a little fat + chopped leftovers + seasoning. Finish with a fried egg or a spoon of yogurt.

Bake:
Leftover potatoes or noodles + vegetables + milk + bouillon + mustard. Top with crumbs and bake until crisp.

4-day mini plan:

Day 1: *Krustenbrot* (page 28) + *Einfache Gemüsesuppe* (page 32) (bake extra bread).

Day 2: Leftover soup for lunch. Dinner: *Bratkartoffeln* (page 72) + fried eggs + *Schneller Rahmspinat* (page 82) (cook extra potatoes).

Day 3: *Bauernfrühstück* (Hoppel Poppel, page 52) using leftover potatoes. Add *Krautsalat* (page 18) or *Gurkensalat* (page 14).

Day 4: *Senfeier mit Kartoffeln* (page 66). Dessert option: *Kaiserschmarrn* (page 92) or Apple Pudding Cake (page 86).

Store it, then use it:

- Portion into meal-sized containers.
- Label soups with the date; use within 3 to 4 days or freeze.
- Freeze bread as slices and pancakes flat for easy grab-and-go.

Salads

PREP TIME:
5 min

CHILL TIME:
2 hr

TOTAL TIME:
2 hr 5 min

MAKES:
2–3 servings

Bohnensalat

Green Bean Salad

When my *mutti* wanted to make a quick salad, she took a can or two of green beans and some simple pantry items and mixed them together with a simple vinaigrette. *Ratze fatze. Bohnensalat* done. Or, take a few extra minutes and thaw frozen beans or cook some fresh beans. Still super quick. I've used frozen beans in my recipe, but see the Tips for how to use fresh or canned.

BUDGET TIP:

Use whatever beans are cheapest, whether frozen, canned, or fresh. This salad is all about the simple vinegar dressing, so it still tastes right even with pantry beans.

INGREDIENTS:

1 lb (454 g)
frozen green beans, *thawed (see Tips)*

¼ cup (38 g)
finely diced onion

3 tbsp (45 ml) vinegar *(see Tips)*

2 tbsp (30 ml)
sunflower or olive oil

2 tsp (8 g)
granulated sugar

1 tsp (6 g) salt,
or to taste

pinch summer savory *(optional)*

pinch fresh ground
black pepper

INSTRUCTIONS:

1. Put the green beans and onions into a serving bowl.
2. Whisk the remaining ingredients together. Pour over the green beans and toss thoroughly to mix.
3. Cover and place in the fridge for several hours to marinate.
4. Let the salad come to room temperature before serving. Check the seasonings and adjust if necessary.

TIPS:

Leave the green beans whole or cut into bite-sized pieces.

Substitute with canned green beans: drain well and use.

Substitute with fresh green beans: trim the ends and cut them into 1-inch pieces. Cook in lightly salted boiling water for about 5 minutes until just tender. Drain, cool, and use.

Substitute yellow wax beans for the green beans or use a combination of the two.

Use your favorite vinegar: red or white wine vinegar, cider vinegar, etc.

Summer savory is the traditional herb used with green beans. This can be substituted with oregano, thyme, dill, or parsley.

PREP TIME:
10 min

TOTAL TIME:
10 min

MAKES:
4 servings

Gurkensalat

Cucumber Salad

This version of *gurkensalat*, unlike my *mutti's*, is made without sour cream or yogurt, so it's perfect for a buffet table or to take along for picnics. It's become one of our favorites, so delightfully refreshing, especially on hot summer days. It's a perfect side dish for almost any meal.

BUDGET TIP:

Skip the fresh dill if it's pricey and use dried dill instead. This salad still tastes bright and classic, and it's a great way to use up cucumbers before they go soft in the fridge.

INGREDIENTS:

2 cucumbers, *peeled and thinly sliced*

4 tbsp (60 ml) white vinegar

4 tbsp (60 ml) water

1–2 tbsp (13–26 g) granulated sugar

½ tsp (3 g) salt

1½ tsp (2.5 g) fresh dill weed, *or to taste*

INSTRUCTIONS:

1. Put the thinly sliced cucumbers into a serving bowl.
2. In a separate bowl, mix together the vinegar, water, sugar, and salt. Pour the dressing over the cucumbers.
3. Sprinkle with dill and stir. Serve.

TIPS:

Instead of vinegar, use lemon juice. YUM!

Add some thinly sliced onions.

If you have tender-skinned English cucumbers, they do not have to be peeled.

Use ½ teaspoon (0.5 gram) dried dill weed instead of fresh.

Use your favorite vinegar: white wine vinegar, cider vinegar, etc.

PREP TIME:
10 min

TOTAL TIME:
10 min

MAKES:
4 servings

Karotten-Apfel-Salat
Carrot Apple Salad

When traditional salad ingredients, such as lettuce and tomatoes, are missing from your crisper, but you have a couple of carrots and an apple, you've got everything you need for a scrumptious *karotten-apfel-salat.*

For added zing, top with some orange zest.

BUDGET TIP:

Buy carrots in a big bag and use up the last few in this salad. No orange juice? Apple juice with a splash of lemon tastes just as fresh.

INGREDIENTS:

3 large carrots

1 large apple

1 cup (240 ml)
orange juice

2 tbsp (30 ml)
white wine vinegar

3 tbsp (45 ml)
sunflower oil

salt and freshly ground
black pepper, *to taste*

1 tsp (1 g)
dried dill weed
(optional)

1 tbsp (21 g)
honey *(optional)*

parsley or dill,
to garnish

INSTRUCTIONS:

1. Peel and shred the carrots and apple. Place into a large serving bowl.
2. In a separate bowl, mix together the orange juice, vinegar, and oil. Pour over the veggies and mix gently.
3. Season with salt and pepper.
4. If desired, mix in dill weed and/or honey. Garnish with parsley or dill to serve.
5. Serve immediately or refrigerate until needed.

TIP:

Use 1 tablespoon (1 gram) minced fresh dill weed instead of dried in the salad.

PREP TIME:
15 min

MARINATE TIME:
1 hr

TOTAL TIME:
1 hr 15 min

MAKES:
4–6 servings

Krautsalat

Cabbage Salad

There's just something about those house salads in Germany that are refreshingly tart and a touch sweet. That's what makes this simple cabbage salad so delicious. You can keep it simple or add some crispy bacon bits. And the caraway seeds add a classic Bavarian touch.

BUDGET TIP:

Cabbage is one of the cheapest veggies around, and this salad really stretches it. Make a double batch because it keeps well for easy sides all week.

INGREDIENTS:

1 lb (454 g) white or green cabbage

2 cups (480 ml) hot water

1 tbsp (18 g) salt

¼ cup (37.5 g) finely diced onions *(optional)*

2 tbsp (30 ml) white wine vinegar

1½ tbsp (22.5 ml) olive oil

1 tsp (2 g) caraway seeds

sugar, salt, and freshly ground black pepper, *to taste*

INSTRUCTIONS:

1. Shred the cabbage into a large bowl. Mix the hot water and salt and pour it over the cabbage. Thoroughly mix it all together and let the cabbage sit for 1 hour, stirring occasionally.
2. Drain the cabbage in a colander, rinse it with water, and press to remove as much liquid as possible.
3. Put the cabbage into a serving bowl and stir in the onions.
4. Mix the vinegar, oil, and caraway seeds together. Pour the dressing over the cabbage and stir.
5. Season with sugar, salt, and pepper. Serve.

Breads

PREP TIME:
1 hr 10 min

RISE TIME:
1 hr

BAKE TIME:
20 min

TOTAL TIME:
2 hr 30 min

MAKES:
8 buns

Heidi's Brötchen

Heidi's Bread Rolls

When traveling to any part of Germany, at least one visit to a bakery is a must. Making these bread rolls fresh at home is the next best thing!

BUDGET TIP:

Homemade *brötchen* use basic pantry staples, so you can skip the cost of bakery rolls. Bake a big batch and freeze extras for quick fresh rolls anytime.

INGREDIENTS:

4 cups (520 g) bread flour *(or all-purpose), divided*

1 tsp (6 g) salt

2¼ tsp (7 g) instant yeast

1¼ cups (300 ml) lukewarm water

water in a spray bottle

TIPS:

Weighing the flour is best. If you don't have a scale, be sure to fluff up the flour before spooning it into your measuring cup, then level the flour with the back of a knife.

Try spraying the rolls with salt water: add about 2 teaspoons (10 milliliters) salt to 2 tablespoons (30 milliliters) water.

Right after the rolls are first sprayed with water, sprinkle with different seeds, such as poppy seeds, chia seeds, sesame seeds, sunflower seeds, or pumpkin seeds.

Try substituting whole wheat flour for the all-purpose flour.

INSTRUCTIONS:

1. Put 3½ cups of the flour (455 grams) and the salt into the large bowl of an electric mixer.
2. Stir the yeast into the warm water and pour the mixture over the flour.
3. Using a dough hook, mix the wet and dry ingredients together slowly until the dough holds together, adding the remaining flour, one tablespoon at a time, as needed. Increase the speed and knead for 10 minutes until the dough is elastic and doesn't stick to the side of the bowl.
4. Remove the smooth dough from the bowl and knead it briefly by hand on a lightly floured surface. Oil the bowl and place the dough back in the bowl. Cover the bowl with a kitchen towel and let the dough rest for 1 hour in a warm place.
5. Deflate the dough by punching it down gently, but do not knead it again.
6. Preheat the oven to 465°F (240°C).
7. Divide the dough into 8 equal parts to form buns, approximately 3.5 ounces (100 grams) each. Place each piece of dough on a parchment paper-lined baking tray and score deeply, using a razor blade or sharp knife.
8. Cover the rolls with a clean kitchen towel and let rise for ½ an hour.
9. Score the risen rolls deeply again and spray lightly with water. Bake in the preheated oven for 10 minutes.
10. Lower the temperature to 410°F (210°C) and spray the rolls with water again. Bake another 10 minutes.
11. Remove when done and let them cool slightly. They can be eaten warm or at room temperature.

PREP TIME:
1 hr

RISE TIME:
1 hr 15 min

BAKE TIME:
15 min

TOTAL TIME:
2 hr 30 min

MAKES:
12 pretzels or
10 rolls

Brezeln & Laugenbrötchen

Pretzels & Pretzel Rolls

Crispy and salty on the outside, yet soft and chewy on the inside, pretzels and pretzel rolls make a delicious snack that pairs perfectly with beer, or serve them as a side to any Bavarian meal. Now, this recipe may look long and complicated, but these pretzels and rolls are quite easy to make.

Traditionally, a lye bath is used to give the crust the right color and taste. However, using a ***baked*** baking soda bath is a lot safer and easier to do. The result? These are really, really close cousins to the ones found in Germany. You'll definitely want to make these over and over again. They are THAT good!

TIP:

Brush the pretzels or rolls with melted butter right after they come out of the oven for extra yumminess.

INGREDIENTS:

6 tbsp (108 g) baking soda

½ cup (120 ml) lukewarm water

1 tsp (4 g) granulated sugar

1 tbsp (10 g) active dry yeast

¾ cup (180 ml) lukewarm milk

2 tbsp (28 g) soft butter

3 cups (390 g) all-purpose flour, *plus more if needed*

1 tsp (6 g) salt

3 cups (720 ml) hot water coarse sea salt, *to sprinkle*

INSTRUCTIONS:

1. Preheat the oven to 250°F (120°C). Line a baking sheet with foil and spread the baking soda in a thin, even layer. Bake for one hour. Meanwhile, make the pretzel dough. Once the soda has baked, remove from the oven and set aside to cool.
2. Prepare two baking sheets by lining them with parchment paper and set aside.
3. Add the water and sugar into a large mixing bowl with a dough hook attachment. Mix in the yeast and let stand for 10 minutes until bubbly. Add the milk and stir.
4. Blend the butter, flour, and salt into the yeast mixture. Let the dough hook knead the dough for 5 to 10 minutes, adding more flour as needed until the dough forms a ball that is smooth, elastic, and not sticky.
5. Cover the bowl with a towel and let the dough rise for 45 to 60 minutes in a warm, draft-free area until doubled in size.
6. Preheat the oven to 425°F (218°C).

TO MAKE PRETZELS:

1. Divide the dough into 12 equal pieces.
2. Roll each piece into an 18-inch long rope, keeping the center thicker than the ends.
3. Form each one into a U shape. Cross the ends of the rope over each other twice about 3 inches from the end. Fold the ends down and press to the curved part at the 4-o'clock and 8-o'clock positions.

TO MAKE ROLLS:

1. Divide the dough into 10 equal pieces.
2. Roll each piece into a ball.

TO PROOF, BATHE, AND BAKE:

1. Place the pretzels and/or rolls onto the parchment-lined baking sheets. Cover with a towel and let rise 15 minutes. Remove the towel and let the dough rise another 15 minutes, letting the surface dry to form a slight skin.
2. Prepare the soda bath. Pour the hot water into a large glass bowl and gradually whisk in the cooled baked baking soda until it's dissolved.
3. One at a time, dip the pretzels and/or rolls into the soda bath for about 3 seconds for the pretzels and 3 seconds per side for the rolls. Place them back on the parchment-lined baking sheets.
4. Slit the rolls and/or the thick center of the pretzels with a sharp knife or razor blade and sprinkle with sea salt.
5. Bake for about 15 minutes until nicely browned. Remove to a wire rack to cool. Best enjoyed while still warm.

TIPS:

If you have sensitive skin, use gloves when dipping the pretzels or rolls. If you want a chewier crust, dip them into the soda bath for a few seconds longer.

For a deeper color, mix 1 egg yolk with 1 tablespoon (15 milliliters) water and brush it over the pretzels or rolls before sprinkling them with salt.

BUDGET TIP:

Pretzels feel like a treat, but they're made from cheap basics like flour, yeast, and baking soda. Make a double batch and freeze, then reheat for a bakery-style snack at home.

PREP TIME:
15 min

RISE TIME:
12 hr

BAKE TIME:
45 min

TOTAL TIME:
13 hr

MAKES:
1 loaf

Krustenbrot

Artisan Bread

This *krustenbrot* is so simple, ANYONE can make it! What's really amazing is how much this tastes like the fresh *brötchen* we'd get at the bakeries in Germany.

With its wonderful crispy, thick crust (after all, *krustenbrot* translates as crust bread) and a chewy crumb, you'll be proud to say, "*I made it all by myself!*"

BUDGET TIP:

Krustenbrot is one of the cheapest artisan-style breads since it's made from just flour, yeast, water, and salt. Use leftover whey from making quark instead of water for extra flavor at no extra cost.

INGREDIENTS:

3 cups (390 g) bread flour

1½ tsp (5 g) instant yeast

1½ cups (360 ml) warm water

1 tsp (6 g) salt

extra flour for dusting

INSTRUCTIONS:

1. Line a Dutch oven (or 6 to 8-quart heavy covered pot) with parchment paper and set aside.
2. Mix the first four ingredients together in a large bowl. The dough will be sticky.
3. Cover the bowl tightly with plastic wrap and let the dough rise at room temperature for 12 to 18 hours.
4. Take the parchment paper out of the Dutch oven and place it on the counter.
5. Sprinkle some flour on the paper and counter. Gently place the dough on the floured counter. Gently fold the dough over itself into thirds, shaping it into a loaf. Place the loaf on the parchment paper. Cover it with a large bowl, plastic wrap, or a clean dish towel to rest.
6. Put the Dutch oven, including the lid, into the oven. Turn the oven to 450°F (230°C) to preheat for 30 minutes.
7. Slash the top of the loaf with a sharp knife or baker's lame *(pronounced "lahm" — a special razor blade bakers use to score bread before baking)*. Remove the preheated Dutch oven and carefully lift the parchment paper with the loaf into it and cover with the hot lid. Return it to the oven.
8. Bake at 450°F (230°C) for 30 minutes. Remove the lid and continue baking for another 15 minutes or until the bread is golden brown.
9. Let the bread cool on a wire rack for at least 1 hour before slicing.

TIP:

As an alternative, replace half the flour with whole wheat flour.

Soups

PREP TIME:
10 min

COOK TIME:
10 min

TOTAL TIME:
20 min

MAKES:
10–12 servings

Einfache Gemüsesuppe

Easy Vegetable Soup

This *einfache gemüsesuppe* is quickly made using frozen vegetables and any leftovers you might have. It's one of my favorite vegetable soup recipes, one I came up with one day when I needed to make room in my freezer. I had a big 5-pound bag of California-style veggies that had been sitting there a long time. Out of the freezer it came and into the soup pot it went. What a nourishing way to clean out your freezer and fridge!

BUDGET TIP:

This is the ultimate clean-out-the-freezer soup using frozen veggies, bouillon, and hot water. Stretch it further by thickening with instant mashed potato flakes or a grated raw potato.

INGREDIENTS:

5 lb (2.3 kg) frozen California-style veggies *(carrots, broccoli, and cauliflower mix)*

about 12 cups (2.9 L) hot or boiling water, *divided*

6 vegetable bouillon cubes *(enough to make 6 cups (1.4 L) broth)*

instant mashed potato flakes, *to taste*

salt and freshly ground black pepper, *to taste*

INSTRUCTIONS:

1. Place the frozen veggies in a large soup pot and add about 11 cups (2.6 L) of hot or boiling water.
2. Dissolve the bouillon cubes in 1 cup (240 milliliters) boiling water and add it to the pot.
3. Bring to a boil, reduce the heat, and cover. Let the soup simmer for about 6 to 10 minutes, or until the veggies are tender.
4. Using a potato masher, crush some of the veggies to make a creamier soup.
5. Stir in enough instant mashed potato flakes to make the soup as creamy and thick as you wish.
6. Season with salt and pepper, and serve.

TIPS:

These quantities are all optional. Use this method with whatever veggies you have on hand. If you have any cooked veggies sitting in the fridge, add them too.

If you don't have or want to use instant mashed potato flakes, you can cut up some raw potatoes or grate them into the soup along with the frozen veggies.

To add some German flavor, season with MAGGI liquid seasoning and/or VEGETA food seasoning.

To add a bit of richness, add a tablespoon or two of butter when you are stirring in the potato flakes.

If you like a bit of spice, add in some Montreal steak spice.

PREP TIME:
5 min

COOK TIME:
10 min

TOTAL TIME:
15 min

MAKES:
4 servings

Flädlesuppe

Pancake Soup

A delicious Bavarian dish, pancake soup is a simple yet comforting soup that makes for a wonderful appetizer. With thin and savory crepe-like pancakes for noodles served in a hot broth and garnished with fresh herbs, it's a real treat.

BUDGET TIP:

Flädlesuppe is a perfect pantry meal since the *Flädle* use basic flour, egg, and milk. Stretch the soup with any broth you have and toss in leftover veggies to make it a full dinner.

INGREDIENTS:

½ cup (65 g) all-purpose flour

1 pinch salt

1 large egg

½ cup (120 ml) milk

1 tbsp (14 g) butter or (15 ml) oil, *plus more if needed*

4 cups (960 ml) beef, chicken, or vegetable broth

chopped fresh parsley or chives, *to garnish*

INSTRUCTIONS:

1. Mix the flour, salt, egg, and milk together in a bowl, making a fairly liquid batter.
2. Melt the butter in a non-stick saucepan. Pour a couple of spoonfuls of batter and immediately swirl and tilt the pan so that the batter forms a thin layer over the bottom.
3. Fry until lightly golden, just a few minutes, then flip and fry the other side for about 30 seconds. Remove the pancake to a plate and repeat with the remaining batter. (You may need to add a bit more butter.) Set the pancakes aside to cool.
4. Heat the broth to a simmer. Adjust the seasonings, if needed (see Tips below).
5. Roll each pancake and cut it into thin slices. Place the rolled-up slices in the bottom of each bowl (usually 1 pancake each).
6. Pour the hot broth over top, garnish with parsley or chives, and serve immediately.

TIPS:

Season the broth with MAGGI liquid seasoning, nutmeg, and/or freshly ground black pepper.

Cook julienned veggies, such as carrots, celery root, or leeks in the broth first. Or steam veggies separately and add them to the finished soup.

Add little pieces of leftover meat.

PREP TIME:
5 min

COOK TIME:
10 min

TOTAL TIME:
15 min

MAKES:
3 servings

Gebrannte Grießsuppe

Roasted CREAM OF WHEAT Soup

I know it may sound strange, but *gebrannte grießsuppe* is so easy, so inexpensive, and so delicious! It's what my boys had when I needed to make a quick lunch. And it's what my *mutti* made for us when we weren't feeling well and had trouble keeping food in our tummies. The CREAM OF WHEAT is pan-roasted in butter, which brings out the nuttiness of the wheat. *Lecker!*

BUDGET TIP:

This soup is one of the cheapest comfort meals, made from bouillon, water, butter, and a few spoonfuls of cereal. Buy CREAM OF WHEAT in the big box and add croutons made from stale bread for a more filling lunch.

INGREDIENTS:

2 bouillon cubes

4 cups (960 ml) boiling water

2 tbsp (28 g) butter

6 tbsp (66 g) CREAM OF WHEAT *(not instant)*

salt, *to taste*

INSTRUCTIONS:

1. Dissolve the bouillon cubes in the boiling water to make a broth and set aside.
2. Melt the butter over medium heat in a medium-sized pot.
3. Stir in the CREAM OF WHEAT and continue stirring as it cooks, letting it slowly turn golden brown or darker (see Tips).
4. Remove the pot from the burner. Carefully add the hot broth, stirring continually.
5. Return the pot to the burner and bring to a boil, stirring continually. Reduce the heat and let it simmer for 5 minutes.
6. Season with salt and serve immediately.

TIPS:

You need to be careful not to let the CREAM OF WHEAT burn. Keep stirring until it is nicely browned. Watch for the steam/smoke that will billow out of the pan the moment the liquid is added. I always turn the stove fan on high to be ready for this.

Season with nutmeg or sweet paprika. Garnish with chopped parsley or chives.

Add croutons to the soup. Cut 2 slices of bread into 1-inch cubes. Heat 2 tablespoons (28 grams) butter in a frying pan and add the bread cubes. Keep stirring until the bread cubes are nicely browned.

PREP TIME:
20 min

COOK TIME:
1 hr 20 min

TOTAL TIME:
1 hr 40 min

MAKES:
6 servings

Hühner-Nudelsuppe

Chicken Noodle Soup *(& Homemade Chicken Broth!)*

Make my easy chicken noodle soup recipe, aka *hühner-nudelsuppe*, made from scratch! Yes, you could make this using store-bought chicken broth. But why pay more for something that doesn't taste as great as homemade?

Buy the least expensive chicken you can—whole or parts—and simmer with soup veggies to make a stock that's really flavorful. Then, make your soup.

BUDGET TIP:

A rotisserie chicken makes this soup extra budget-friendly because you get meat plus a flavorful carcass for broth. Add inexpensive veggies and egg noodles, then freeze leftovers in portions for quick meals later.

INGREDIENTS: FOR THE CHICKEN BROTH:

1 whole chicken, *cut into pieces*

5–6 cups (1.2–1.4 L) water

1 tsp (3 g) VEGETA food seasoning *(see Tips below)*

½ tsp (1 g) freshly ground black pepper

1–2 celery ribs, *chopped*

1 onion, *quartered*

1–2 carrots, *chopped*

1–2 parsnips, *chopped*

1–2 leeks, *chopped*

½ celeriac, *chopped (optional)*

INSTRUCTIONS: FOR THE CHICKEN BROTH:

1. Remove any visible fat from the chicken.
2. Put the chicken pieces into a large pot and cover with water.
3. Add the remaining ingredients and bring to a boil. Reduce the heat, cover, and simmer for about 1 hour, until the chicken is tender. Occasionally skim the foam from the top while the broth is simmering.
4. Remove the chicken pieces and set aside. Strain the cooking liquid through a sieve, saving the liquid and discarding the vegetables.
5. Return the broth to the pot to make the soup, or let it cool to refrigerate or freeze for later use.
6. Once the chicken has cooled, remove the meat from the bones. Save the meat pieces for a future meal, or use immediately.

FOR THE CHICKEN NOODLE SOUP:

5 cups (1.2 L) homemade chicken broth *(from above)*

2 celery ribs, *sliced*

2 carrots, *sliced*

1 onion, *chopped*

1–1½ cups (38–57 g) egg noodles

1–2 cups (150–300 g) diced cooked chicken

CONT'D

FOR THE CHICKEN NOODLE SOUP:

1. Pour the broth into a large pot. Add the vegetables and bring to a boil. Reduce the heat and simmer until the vegetables are almost tender, about 15 minutes.
2. Add the egg noodles and simmer for about 8 to 10 minutes, until the noodles are tender.
3. Add the chicken to the soup and season with VEGETA, salt, and pepper.
4. Garnish with parsley to serve.

VEGETA food seasoning, *to taste*

salt and freshly ground black pepper, *to taste*

chopped fresh parsley, *to garnish*

TIPS:

When making the soup, you can also add mushrooms, cauliflower, broccoli, peppers, etc. Each additional vegetable adds a different flavor to the finished soup—each absolutely delicious. Plus it's a great way to clean out the veggie drawer!

For a deeper flavor, remove the chicken when it is tender. Separate the meat from the bones and return the bones to the pot. Simmer for up to another 4 hours, then continue with the recipe.

If you don't have VEGETA, use about 1 teaspoon salt and some freshly ground pepper.

Instead of egg noodles, you can use pasta. Small shapes work best, and the kids love them.

Turn this easy chicken noodle soup recipe into a chicken rice soup: add about ¾ cup of long-grained rice with the veggies and simmer for about 20 to 25 minutes.

Use a carcass from a cooked rotisserie chicken instead (perhaps several that you've frozen) to make the broth. You may need to add a bit of concentrated chicken stock to amplify the flavor.

PREP TIME:
5 min

COOK TIME:
30 min

TOTAL TIME:
35 min

MAKES:
6 servings

Karottensuppe

Carrot Soup

This *karottensuppe* will probably become one of your favorites. Why? Because it's just so *wunderbar*! With plenty of carrots, potatoes, and chunks of meat, this hearty soup is filling and nutritious. I prefer to use frozen sliced carrots to make quick work of this delicious soup.

BUDGET TIP:

Carrots, potatoes, and onions make this soup filling without costing much. To save even more, omit the meat entirely and use bouillon for flavor, then thicken with instant mashed potato flakes.

INGREDIENTS:

1 lb (454 g) beef brisket or other meat, *cubed (optional)*

2 lb (908 g) frozen sliced carrots

2 lb (908 g) potatoes, *peeled and cubed*

1 medium onion, *chopped*

1–2 tbsp (9–18 g) VEGETA food seasoning

1 bay leaf

salt and freshly ground black pepper, *to taste*

MAGGI liquid seasoning, *to taste*

INSTRUCTIONS:

1. Place the meat, carrots, potatoes, and onions in a large soup pot. Add enough water to cover the meat and veggies. Add the VEGETA and bay leaf.
2. Bring to a boil. Reduce the heat to a simmer, cover, and cook for about 30 to 60 minutes, until the meat is cooked. The longer you let it cook, the more flavorful the soup will become.
3. Season with salt, pepper, and MAGGI, and serve.

TIPS:

Season with celery seeds and parsley, to taste, for extra flavor.

If you don't have VEGETA, just add about 1 teaspoon (6 grams) salt and some freshly ground black pepper to start. Adjust seasonings, to taste.

If you want extra flavor and don't mind a bit of extra work, brown the meat first in a bit of oil and sauté the onions.

Substitute fresh carrots for the frozen, cutting them into ¼-inch slices.

Instead of using raw meat, try some sausage, kielbasa, or wieners. You will only need to cook the soup until the veggies are tender, about 10 to 15 minutes.

If you would like a thicker and creamier soup, slowly add just enough instant mashed potato flakes, stirring constantly, until it is as thick as you like. Adding a grated raw potato in the beginning is another way to thicken the soup.

PREP TIME:
10 min

COOK TIME:
30 min

TOTAL TIME:
40 min

MAKES:
4–6 servings

Kohlsuppe mit Kartoffeln
Potato & Cabbage Soup

This *kohlsuppe mit kartoffeln* is so delicious on a cool autumn evening or a cold snowy day. It's perfect for a nice light lunch or dinner served with some crusty German bread. If you prefer a more hearty meal, add a can of beans or some meat, like smoked sausages or wieners.

BUDGET TIP:

This soup is a budget classic made from low-cost veggies and broth. Keep it meatless to save money, and stretch it with a can of beans if you want it extra hearty.

INGREDIENTS:

1 lb (454 g) green or savoy cabbage, *shredded*

1 lb (454 g) potatoes, *peeled and cubed*

½ lb (227 g) carrots, *sliced*

½ lb (227 g) leeks, *sliced*

1 small onion, *diced*

6 cups (1.4 L) vegetable broth

salt and freshly ground black pepper, *to taste*

chopped fresh parsley, *to garnish*

INSTRUCTIONS:

1. Put the cabbage, potatoes, carrots, leeks, onions, and broth in a large soup pot. Bring to a boil.
2. Reduce the heat to low and simmer for about 30 minutes, or until all the veggies are tender. Season with salt and pepper.
3. Sprinkle with parsley to serve.

TIPS:

For more flavor, first brown the cabbage and onion in some olive oil over medium-high heat. Then add the rest of the veggies and broth and continue as above.

Purée half the soup for a creamier version.

If you would like to make this soup even heartier, brown 1 pound (454 grams) of ground beef along with the cabbage and onions before adding everything else.

Add smoked sausages or kielbasa to the soup as it is simmering.

Serve with a dollop of sour cream and a sprinkle of crispy bacon pieces. Yum!

Season with VEGETA food seasoning and/or MAGGI liquid seasoning.

Adding a little bit of vinegar and some caraway seeds is also delicious.

PREP TIME:
10 min

COOK TIME:
25 min

TOTAL TIME:
35 min

MAKES:
8–10 servings

Linsensuppe

Lentil Soup

Looking for a vegan *linsensuppe* that's easy to make? Here's one that you'll make in about 30 minutes.

I didn't even know about it being vegan when I used to make this years ago. I just made it 'cause I loved it!

BUDGET TIP:

Skip the leek *(it's optional anyway)* and use an extra onion instead. If you want that leek flavor, toss in a pinch of dried onion flakes or a little garlic powder. Same hearty taste, less on your grocery bill.

INGREDIENTS:

2 tbsp (30 ml) oil

1 medium onion, *chopped*

2 stalks celery, *chopped*

1 leek, *finely chopped (optional)*

2 large carrots, *chopped*

2–4 potatoes, *chopped*

2 cups (400 g) dried red lentils

10 cups (2.4 L) vegetable stock

2 bay leaves

salt and freshly ground pepper, *to taste*

INSTRUCTIONS:

1. Heat the oil in a large soup pot. Add the onions, celery and leeks. Cook over high heat for about 5 minutes, stirring occasionally.
2. Add the remaining ingredients.
3. Reduce the header, cover, and simmer for about 20 minutes or until the vegetables are tender.
4. Remove the bay leaves.
5. If you wish, use an immersion blender to mash up the veggies.
6. Season with salt and pepper, and serve.

Mains

PREP TIME:
10 min

COOK TIME:
12 min

TOTAL TIME:
22 min

MAKES:
4 servings

Arme Ritter

German French Toast

This German French toast is a traditional *arme ritter* recipe that will remind you of sitting around *Oma's* table. Make these as a delicious way to use up stale bread and serve them with cinnamon-sugar sprinkled over the top!

BUDGET TIP:

Arme ritter uses simple pantry basics like bread, eggs, and milk, so it's perfect for using up stale bread. Keep it simple with just sugar or syrup so it feels special without extra cost.

INGREDIENTS:

2 large eggs

⅛ tsp (0.75 g) salt

2 tbsp (26 g) sugar

1 tsp (2 g) grated lemon zest *(optional)*

1 cup (240 ml) milk *(part cream if desired)*

½ lb (227 g) loaf of stale bread, *½-inch to ¾-inch thick slices*

3–4 tbsp (42–56 g) butter

INSTRUCTIONS:

1. Preheat the oven to 200°F (93°C), if you want to keep the *arme ritter* warm until all are fried.
2. Place a sheet of wax or parchment paper on the countertop.
3. Mix the eggs, salt, sugar, lemon zest, and milk in a bowl.
4. Dip both sides of each bread slice into the egg mixture.
5. Let the bread slices sit for a few minutes on the wax-paper to let the egg mixture soak in.
6. Meanwhile, heat the butter in a frying pan or griddle.
7. Fry the bread slices in batches, until golden brown, about 2 to 3 minutes per side.
8. Remove the fried slices from the pan and transfer them to a cookie sheet. Place the cookie sheet in the oven to keep warm until all of the bread slices have been fried.
9. Serve with fruit sauce, syrup, or simply sprinkled with powdered sugar or cinnamon sugar.

TIPS:

For the cinnamon sugar, stir together 1 tablespoon (9 grams) cinnamon with 4 tablespoons (52 grams) granulated sugar.

The best type of bread to use is brioche, French baguette, or challah. However, almost any bread will work. Just make sure it's stale so it can soak up the egg mixture. The texture may not be perfect, but it will still taste awesome!

PREP TIME:
5 min

COOK TIME:
15 min

TOTAL TIME:
20 min

MAKES:
4 servings

Bauernfrühstück

Hoppel Poppel

Hoppel poppel is a traditional way to use up leftovers in Berlin. Made with meat, potatoes, onions, and eggs, it's one of those great quick recipes for supper or lunch. It's one of my favorite potato recipes that I remember from *Mutti*.

BUDGET TIP:

Hoppel poppel is made from leftovers, so it's a budget hero. Use leftover potatoes and whatever cooked meat you have, or skip the meat and add any veggies, such as mushrooms, peppers, or onions, to stretch it further.

INGREDIENTS:

about 1 lb (454 g) leftover cooked meat

about 1½ lb (681 g) leftover boiled potatoes

1–2 onions, *chopped*

4 tbsp (56 g) butter or (60 ml) olive oil, *divided*

salt and freshly ground pepper, *to taste*

6–8 eggs

INSTRUCTIONS:

1. Cut the meat and potatoes into slices.
2. In a large skillet, fry the onions in 2 tablespoons (28 g) butter. Once the onions are translucent, add the meat.
3. Add the remaining 2 tablespoons (28 g) butter, then add the potatoes.
4. Continue frying until the potatoes are golden brown.
5. Season with salt and pepper.
6. Beat the eggs and pour them over the meat and potatoes. Stir gently until the eggs are set. Serve immediately.

TIPS:

Use boiled or roasted beef, pork, chicken, hamburgers, lamb —whatever you have.

Sprinkle with fresh parsley to serve.

PREP TIME:
20 min

COOK TIME:
30 min

TOTAL TIME:
50 min

MAKES:
6–8 servings

Gemüsefrittata

Vegetable Frittata

This frittata recipe is simply too delicious not to include. With its German twist, this *gemüsefrittata* makes a perfect light supper, much like a quiche.

BUDGET TIP:

Frittata is a cheap, clean-out-the-fridge meal. Use fewer eggs by adding more potatoes or veggies, perhaps a sprinkle of cheese, then slice leftovers into wedges for tomorrow's lunch.

INGREDIENTS:

3 tbsp (45 ml) oil

2 medium zucchini, *cut into bite-sized chunks*

2 large red peppers, *cut into bite-sized chunks*

4 medium cooked potatoes, *peeled and cubed*

¾ lb (340 g) mixed vegetables *(squash, broccoli, leeks, etc.), cut into bite-sized chunks*

1½ tsp (9 g) salt, *plus more to taste*

8 large eggs

¾ cup (180 ml) cream

freshly ground black pepper, *to taste*

3 tbsp (9 g) chopped fresh basil

⅓ lb (150 g) grated German cheese *(like Emmental or Butterkäse)*

INSTRUCTIONS:

1. Preheat the oven to 400°F (205°C).
2. In a large oven-safe saucepan or deep skillet, heat the oil over medium heat.
3. Add the zucchini, peppers, potatoes, and mixed vegetables. Sauté for about 5 to 7 minutes, stirring occasionally, until slightly tender. Season with the salt.
4. In a bowl, whisk together the eggs, cream, pepper, basil, and grated cheese.
5. Pour the egg mixture evenly over the sautéed vegetables in the pan.
6. Transfer the pan to the preheated oven and bake for 20 to 25 minutes, or until the eggs are fully set and lightly golden on top.
7. Let rest for 5 minutes before slicing and serving.

PREP TIME:
10 min

COOK TIME:
30 min

TOTAL TIME:
40 min

MAKES:
4 servings

Hühnerfrikassee

Chicken Fricassee

Make this *hühnerfrikassee* and you'll think you're back in *Oma's* kitchen. With as many variations as there are German omas, it was often a meal that consisted of leftover veggies and anything else found in the fridge. Now it graces the best restaurant menus.

Made with humble ingredients like chicken and hearty vegetables simmered in a simple yet rich and creamy white sauce, this delicious dish truly is one of the best comfort foods.

BUDGET TIP:

Use rotisserie chicken or leftover cooked chicken instead of buying fresh meat—it will still taste rich and traditional. Stretch the creamy sauce with a little extra broth and frozen peas so it feeds more for less.

INGREDIENTS:

1 tbsp (15 ml) olive oil

3 tbsp (42 g) butter, *divided*

8 oz (227 g) white or cremini mushrooms, *thickly sliced*

1½ lb (681 g) boneless skinless chicken thighs, *cubed*

4 tbsp (32 g) all-purpose flour

2 cups (480 ml) hot chicken broth

1 cup (140 g) frozen peas, *thawed (optional)*

½ cup (120 ml) heavy cream or 10%

salt and freshly ground black pepper, *to taste*

fresh parsley, *to garnish*

INSTRUCTIONS:

1. In a large saucepan, heat the oil and 1 tablespoon (14 grams) of butter over medium heat. Add the mushrooms and sauté for several minutes until golden brown. Remove the mushrooms with a slotted spoon and set aside.
2. Add the remaining butter and lightly cook the chicken pieces without browning them. Sprinkle the chicken with flour and stir to mix. Add the hot broth and continue stirring; increase the heat and bring to a boil.
3. Return the mushrooms to the saucepan and stir. Cover, reduce the heat to medium-low, and simmer for about 15 to 20 minutes. If the sauce gets too thick, add a bit of extra water.
4. Add the peas and simmer for 2 to 3 minutes. Add the cream, salt, and pepper and stir. Sprinkle with parsley and serve.

TIPS:

Add 1 teaspoon (2.9 grams) capers to the finished sauce.

Add asparagus, cut into 1-inch slices, about 10 minutes before the sauce is finished.

Season with 1 tablespoon (15 milliliters) lemon juice.

Season with paprika and/or nutmeg.

You can substitute the chicken thighs with boneless skinless chicken breasts.

If you prefer a creamy white wine sauce, replace ½ cup (120 milliliters) of the chicken broth with ½ cup (120 milliliters) dry white wine such as Sauvignon Blanc, Riesling, or Pinot Grigio.

Super Quick Chicken Fricassee: Use leftover cooked chicken and follow the above recipe, only the cooking time is reduced to about 5 minutes for the chicken to heat through and the flour to cook.

PREP TIME:
15 min

COOK TIME:
20 min

TOTAL TIME:
35 min

MAKES:
4 servings

Labskaus

Corned Beef Hash

Labskaus may have started as sailor food, but now it's a northern German favorite, especially around Hamburg.

Keep the classics: potatoes, corned beef, beets, and a fried egg. Then make it creamy or chunky, mild or spicy, and if you dare... add a *rollmops* (pickled herring)!

BUDGET TIP:

Labskaus is a perfect stretch-a-pound meal. Use canned corned beef and canned beets (cheap, no waste), and bulk it up with extra potatoes so it feeds more people without tasting like you skimped.

INGREDIENTS:

1½ lbs (681 g) peeled Yukon gold potatoes, *cubed*

1 tsp (6 g) salt, *plus more to taste*

3 tbsp (42 g) butter, *divided*

1 cup (150 g) finely diced onions

1 lb (454 g) canned corned beef, *cubed*

1 cup (157 g) canned diced red beets, *drained and juice reserved*

2 tbsp (30 ml) dill pickle brine

2 tbsp (30 ml) reserved beet juice, *plus more if needed*

freshly ground black pepper, *as needed*

Freshly grated nutmeg, *to taste*

4 large eggs

fresh parsley, *to garnish*

1 cup (170 g) canned sliced pickled red beets, *drained*

2 dill pickles, *thickly sliced*

INSTRUCTIONS:

1. Put the potatoes in a medium saucepan and cover them with water. Add the salt and bring to a boil over high heat. Cover the saucepan, reduce the heat to medium-high, and simmer until the potatoes are tender, about 15 minutes.
2. While the potatoes are cooking, melt 2 tablespoons (28 grams) of the butter in a large skillet over medium heat. Add the onions and sauté for 5 to 7 minutes, stirring frequently, until they are tender but not browned.
3. Add the corned beef and fry for about 2 minutes, stirring occasionally. Stir in the diced beets. Cover the skillet and set it aside until the potatoes are ready.
4. Drain the potatoes and mash them together with the pickle brine and beet juice.
5. Add the mashed potatoes to the beef hash, stir well, and season with salt, pepper, and nutmeg. If the hash is too thick, stir in a bit more beet juice. Cover the skillet to keep the hash warm.
6. In a medium skillet over medium heat, melt the remaining tablespoon (14 grams) of butter and fry the eggs sunny-side up for 2 to 3 minutes.
7. To serve, arrange the hash on plates, place a fried egg on the side, and garnish with the parsley, sliced beets and pickle slices.

TIP:

If you prefer, you can serve poached eggs instead of fried. *Rollmops* (pickled herring fillets) are another traditional garnish. These fillets can also be finely diced and added to the *labskaus* as it is cooking.

PREP TIME:
20 min

COOK TIME:
1 hr 5 min

TOTAL TIME:
1 hr 25 min

MAKES:
4–6 servings

Kartoffelpuffer aus dem Ofen

Baked German Potato Pancake Casserole

Crispy top, creamy middle: my oven-baked *kartoffelpuffer* casserole (*döppekooche*-style) made with grated potatoes, butter, and eggs.

BUDGET TIP:

This baked potato pancake turns raw potatoes into a big, filling meal. Serve it with applesauce or a simple cabbage salad so you get a full dinner without spending extra on meat.

INGREDIENTS:

3 lb (1.36 kg) potatoes, *peeled*

1 small onion, *finely chopped*

¼ cup (32 g) cornstarch or more as needed

2 tsp (12 g) salt

Freshly ground black pepper, *to taste*

3 large eggs

¼ cup (57 g) + 1 tbsp (14 g) butter, *divided*

INSTRUCTIONS:

1. Preheat the oven to 400°F (205°C). Have a 9×13-inch baking dish or a 12-inch cast-iron casserole/skillet ready.
2. Grate the potatoes using the coarse side of a box grater (or a food processor).
3. If the grated potatoes look very wet, wrap them in a clean towel and squeeze out as much liquid as you can.
4. In a large bowl, thoroughly mix the grated potatoes, chopped onion, and cornstarch. If the mixture looks very wet after mixing, add another tablespoon (8 grams) cornstarch.
5. Add the salt, pepper, and eggs, and mix very well—clean hands are easiest.
6. Put ¼ cup (57 grams) butter into the dish and place it in the oven until the butter melts and sizzles, but does not brown.
7. Carefully remove the hot dish from the oven. Add the potato mixture (watch for splatters) and spread it out evenly. Dot the top with the remaining tablespoon (14 grams) butter.
8. Bake for 60 minutes, or until deeply browned on top and set in the center. If the top browns too quickly, loosely cover with foil, then uncover for the last 5 to 10 minutes.

TIPS:

The drier the potato mixture, the crispier the crust and the more set the center.

A 12-inch cast-iron casserole gives a crispier bottom crust than glass or ceramic.

To reheat leftovers, warm slices in a 350°F (175°C) oven or air fryer until hot. Microwaving softens the crust.

PREP TIME:
10 min

COOK TIME:
30 min

TOTAL TIME:
40 min

MAKES:
6 servings

Reisfleisch

One Skillet Rice Dinner

This German rice dish, aka *reisfleisch*, is so quick and easy to make. It is similar to a risotto, but you use regular long grain white rice and add meat as well. You can add diced red or green peppers if you wish.

BUDGET TIP:

This is a great pantry meal with rice and canned veggies, and you can stretch it by using leftover meat or skipping it entirely. Turn leftovers into a quick casserole so nothing goes to waste.

INGREDIENTS:

3 tbsp (45 ml) oil or (42 g) butter

1 onion, *chopped*

2 cups (360 g) white long grain rice, *uncooked*

1 28-oz (800-g) can diced tomatoes, *undrained*

1 10-oz (285-g) can sliced mushrooms, *undrained*

2 cups (480 ml) water, *plus more if needed*

1 tbsp (9 g) VEGETA food seasoning

1 12-oz (340-g) can corned beef, *cut into chunks*

parsley, salt, and freshly ground black pepper, *to taste*

INSTRUCTIONS:

1. Heat the oil in a large saucepan. Add the onion and sauté until softened and slightly browned. Stir in the rice and brown slightly over high heat.
2. Add the tomatoes, mushrooms, and water. Stir in the VEGETA.
3. Cover and simmer over medium-low heat for 15 minutes, stirring occasionally and adding extra water as needed. Add the corned beef and cook until the rice is tender, about 5 minutes more.
4. Season with parsley, salt, and pepper, and serve.

TIPS:

Use salt and pepper if you do not have VEGETA food seasoning.

Add other canned vegetables and/or mushrooms, if desired.

Substitute the corned beef with 2 cups leftover ham or other cooked meat, cut in chunks.

Instead of the canned tomatoes, add a can of tomato sauce.

If you have any leftover gravy, add it.

Omit the meat and serve as a side dish.

PREP TIME:
10 min

COOK TIME:
25 min

TOTAL TIME:
35 min

MAKES:
4–6 servings

Rote-Bete-Suppe mit Stampfkartoffeln

Beet Soup with Mash & Fried Eggs

My sweet hubby is the one who introduced me to this *rote-bete-suppe mit stampfkartoffeln*. He had fond childhood memories of it and taught me how to make it just like his *mutti* did. It's a super easy beet soup with special mashed potatoes served with fried eggs on the side.

BUDGET TIP:

This is mostly potatoes and canned beets, with bacon just for flavor. Save more by skipping the bacon and using veggie broth or water, then add a fried egg to make it a full meal.

INGREDIENTS:

2 lb (908 g) potatoes, *peeled and quartered*

1 tsp (6 g) salt

3 tbsp (42 g) butter, *divided*

¼ lb (113 g) bacon, *diced*

1 onion, *diced*

4 cups (680 g) canned sliced red beets, *drained*

4 cups (960 ml) beef broth

1 tsp (4 g) sugar

1 tbsp (15 ml) vinegar

salt and freshly ground black pepper, *to taste*

1 cup (240 ml) hot milk, *plus more if needed*

1–2 eggs per person

INSTRUCTIONS:

1. Boil the potatoes with the salt until tender, about 20 minutes. Drain and keep warm.
2. Meanwhile, melt 1 tablespoon (14 grams) of butter in a small skillet. Add the bacon and sauté until the fat has rendered, about 5 minutes. Transfer the bacon and fat to a bowl.
3. Add another tablespoon (14 grams) of butter to the skillet and sauté the onions until translucent, about 5 to 7 minutes.
4. Using a blender or food processor, blend together the sautéed onions, beets, and broth until smooth.
5. Pour the puréed soup into a saucepan and bring it to a simmer for 5 minutes. Add the sugar and vinegar. Season with salt and pepper, adding more sugar and/or vinegar, if desired. Cover and keep warm.
6. Mash the potatoes, adding as much milk as needed. Stir in the bacon with the fat (or add butter instead) and season with salt and pepper.
7. Fry the eggs in the remaining tablespoon (14 grams) of butter for 2 to 3 minutes.
8. Serve the soup in bowls and the mashed potatoes and eggs on separate plates, or see *Tips* for a fun alternative.

TIPS:

Here's how we made it a fun meal for our boys: to serve, put a mound of mash on a plate. Using a ladle, make an indentation in the middle of the mound to create a moat for a lake of beet soup, and fill it with soup. Serve the eggs on the side. Now, the goal is to not let the soup leak out of the moat as you eat the mash and soup. The person who keeps the moat intact the longest wins an extra serving of dessert!

If you want to make this meal even faster, use good quality instant mashed potato flakes instead of fresh potatoes. Adding the bacon makes them taste homemade.

PREP TIME:
5 min

COOK TIME:
5 min

TOTAL TIME:
10 min

MAKES:
4 servings

Senfeier mit Kartoffeln

Mustard Sauce with Eggs & Potatoes

Eggs with mustard sauce recipe, aka *eier in senfsosse*! *WUNDERBAR!* It's one of those easy and quick lunch recipes that's very common in Germany, especially in Berlin and Bremen.

BUDGET TIP:

Eggs in mustard sauce are classic comfort food made from low-cost staples. Serve with boiled potatoes or rice and use any leftover herbs or a splash of vinegar to boost flavor without spending more.

INGREDIENTS:

4 tbsp (56 g) butter

4 tbsp (32 g) all-purpose flour

1½ cups (360 ml) vegetable broth

1½ cups (360 ml) milk or cream

3 tbsp (45 ml) mustard

salt and freshly ground black pepper, *to taste*

1 tsp (5 ml) lemon juice, *or to taste*

8 hard-boiled eggs, *cut in half*

chopped fresh parsley, *to garnish*

INSTRUCTIONS:

1. In another saucepan over medium heat, melt the butter and add the flour, stirring constantly.
2. Add the broth and milk slowly, stirring until the sauce is thickened. If it's too thick, add a bit more milk.
3. Add the mustard and season with salt and pepper. Add the lemon juice.
4. Pour the sauce over the halved eggs and garnish with parsley.

TIP:

This is often served with creamed spinach (see page 82) on the side.

Sides

PREP TIME:
15 min

COOK TIME:
45 min

TOTAL TIME:
1 hr

MAKES:
6 servings

Bayerisches Weisskraut

Bavarian Braised Cabbage

Bavarian braised cabbage is a classic side dish often served with pork knuckle, *bratwurst*, or roast chicken. It's similar to *sauerkraut*, which is probably the most common cabbage dish, but if you prefer something milder and less tangy, then this is the cabbage dish for you.

BUDGET TIP:

Use oil instead of bacon fat and swap in vegetable broth (or even water) to keep this dish inexpensive without losing that classic sweet-and-tangy flavor. It's also a great side for stretching meals, since one head of cabbage goes a long way.

INGREDIENTS:

3 tbsp (45 ml) oil or (26 g) bacon fat

1 onion, *thinly sliced*

1 large apple, *peeled & thickly sliced*

2 tbsp (26 g) granulated sugar

1¾ lb (800 g) white or green cabbage, *shredded*

1 garlic clove, *crushed (optional)*

1 tsp (2 g) caraway seeds

1 cup (240 ml) chicken broth, *plus more if needed*

salt and freshly ground black pepper, *to taste*

1 tbsp (15 ml) white wine vinegar

INSTRUCTIONS:

1. In a large skillet, heat the oil over medium-high heat. Add the onions and sauté until lightly caramelized, about 5 minutes. Add the apple slices and sauté for 1 minute.
2. Stir in the sugar and the shredded cabbage. Continue to sauté over medium heat until some of the cabbage is browned as well.
3. Add the garlic, caraway seeds, and broth. Stir to scrape up any browned bits at the bottom of the skillet. Season with salt and pepper.
4. Bring to a boil and reduce the heat to low. Cover and simmer for about a ½ hour, or until the cabbage is tender, stirring occasionally and adding extra broth or water if needed.
5. Stir in the vinegar and season with additional salt, pepper, sugar, and vinegar, if needed. Serve.

TIPS:

To thicken the sauce, dissolve 1 to 2 tablespoons (8 to 16 grams) cornstarch in a bit of cold water. Slowly add just enough to the boiling liquid until thickened.

Use vegetable broth if you're making this vegan. Water can also be substituted for this.

You can substitute with apple cider vinegar, if you wish.

You can decrease or increase the cooking time depending on how tender you like the cabbage.

Add a bay leaf, if desired.

PREP TIME:
10 min

COOK TIME:
15 min

TOTAL TIME:
25 min

MAKES:
4 servings

Bratkartoffeln

Fried Potatoes

Fried potatoes are another classic side dish that is one of my favorites that I grew up on. For the best *bratkartoffeln*, you'll need to cook your potatoes the day before and let them chill in the fridge overnight, because cold potatoes make the best fried potatoes. If you're short on time, check out my ***Tips*** for an alternative method.

BUDGET TIP:

This is the perfect way to turn leftover boiled potatoes into a whole new meal. Skip the bacon if you want to save even more, then top your *bratkartoffeln* with a fried egg to make a filling, budget-friendly supper.

INGREDIENTS:

1¾ lb (794.5 g) cooked potatoes *(see Tips below)*

2 tbsp (28 g) butter

8 slices bacon, *diced (optional)*

1 cup (150 g) diced onion

salt and freshly ground black pepper, *to taste*

INSTRUCTIONS:

1. Cut the potatoes into ¼-inch slices and set aside.
2. In a large skillet, heat the butter and sauté the bacon until golden brown. Remove the crispy bacon pieces with a slotted spoon and set aside. Remove some of the butter/bacon grease, leaving about 2 to 3 tablespoons in the pan. Set the rest aside to use, if needed.
3. Add the potatoes to the fat in the pan and fry over medium-high heat for about 5 minutes before turning to allow the potato slices to brown. Turn, adding the onions and continuing to gently turn as needed. Add more butter/bacon grease, if needed.
4. After the potatoes are browned, add the reserved bacon and season with a little salt and pepper. Serve immediately.

TIPS:

Ideally, make *pellkartoffeln* the day before, which are potatoes boiled in their skins until tender. They are then cooled slightly, peeled, and refrigerated.

What do you do when you want to make *bratkartoffeln*, but you don't have pre-cooked potatoes? Just use raw ones! Peel and slice raw potatoes and proceed with the recipe. You'll just need to let them cook a bit longer. I cover the pan to help speed things up and remove the lid just before they're done so that they crisp up a bit.

Add fresh parsley, chives, and/or other fresh herbs.

Add some leftover meat pieces to the potatoes while they are cooking.

Add more or less onions, as desired. Chopped green onions – tops and bottoms – would also taste great.

PREP TIME:
15 min

COOK TIME:
15 min

TOTAL TIME:
30 min

MAKES:
4 servings

Himmel und Erde

Heaven & Earth

Himmel und erde (heaven and earth) is a mixture of mashed potatoes (from earth) and apples (from heaven).

BUDGET TIP:

Himmel und erde turns low-cost potatoes and apples into a filling meal. Use leftover onions or bacon bits for flavor so you do not need to buy anything extra.

INGREDIENTS:

1 lb (454 g) starchy potatoes

1 lb (454 g) cooking apples

4 tbsp (56 g) butter, *divided*

freshly grated nutmeg, *to taste*

salt, and freshly ground black pepper, *to taste*

1–2 onions, *sliced*

INSTRUCTIONS:

1. Peel and cut the potatoes into 1-inch cubes. Peel and thickly slice the apples.
2. Cook the potatoes and apples in boiling salted water until tender, about 10 to 15 minutes. Drain.
3. While the potatoes and apples are cooking, fry the onion slices in 2 tablespoons (28 grams) butter until they're nice and crispy.
4. Add the remaining 2 tablespoons (28 grams) of butter to the potatoes and apples and mash until smooth and creamy. Season with nutmeg, salt, and pepper.
5. Spoon the fried onions over the mashed mixture and serve it as a main dish or as a hearty side with sausages or other meats.

PREP TIME:
30 min

COOK TIME:
30 min

TOTAL TIME:
1 hr

MAKES:
12 pancakes

Kartoffelpuffer

Potato Pancakes

These potato pancakes will bring back memories of *Oma's* kitchen for sure. Made with grated potatoes and pan fried, these are crispy on the outside and creamy on the inside. They are so delicious sprinkled with sugar or served with applesauce on the side.

BUDGET TIP:

Kartoffelpuffer are made from the cheapest basics—potatoes, onion, and eggs—so they're perfect when the grocery budget is tight. Serve them with applesauce instead of sour cream for an inexpensive, classic German topping that still tastes like childhood.

INGREDIENTS:

5–6 potatoes, *peeled (see Tips)*

3 large eggs

1 small onion, *finely grated (optional)*

1 tsp (6 g) salt

4 tbsp (32 g) all-purpose flour or (40 g) potato starch

butter and oil, *for frying (see Tips)*

TIPS:

I use Yukon Gold potatoes, but any starchy potato will work. Grate the potatoes as fine or as coarse as you wish.

Authentic German potato pancakes call for peeling the potatoes. Keeping the skin on when you have nice new potatoes, though, is healthier and quicker.

Change the quantities as needed. Depending on how little or how much liquid is in your squeezed potatoes, you may need to add an extra egg yolk or more flour.

Use a mixture of butter and oil for frying. Canola oil is great and it keeps the butter from burning.

Add some freshly ground black pepper to the mixture.

INSTRUCTIONS:

1. Preheat the oven to 300°F (150°C). Place a cookie sheet in the oven.
2. Line a plate with paper towels and set aside.
3. Grate the potatoes, either with a box grater or the grating blade of your food processor.
4. Drain the grated potatoes (in batches) by putting them into a clean dish towel and squeezing to remove as much moisture as possible.
5. Put the drained potatoes into a large bowl. Add the eggs, grated onion, salt, and flour. Mix well.
6. Heat some butter and oil in a large skillet over medium-high heat.
7. Using a large spoon, drop tablespoonfuls of the potato mixture into the hot butter/oil mixture. Use the back of the spoon to flatten them out.
8. Fry over medium-high heat until golden brown, about 3 to 4 minutes, then flip them over and continue frying until they're cooked through and crispy brown, about another 3 to 4 minutes. If they are frying too fast, lower the heat to medium.
9. Remove the pancakes to the plate lined with paper towels to remove excess oil and then transfer them to the oven to keep them warm. Continue until all the batter is used up, adding more butter or oil as needed.
10. Serve sprinkled with sugar, or with applesauce or sour cream on the side.

PREP TIME:
10 min

COOK TIME:
1 hr

TOTAL TIME:
1 hr 10 min

MAKES:
6 servings

Rotkohl

Red Cabbage

There's nothing quite like delicious German red cabbage. A classic dish that's the perfect side to just about any German meal. This traditional recipe calls for apples, which give it that wonderful sweet-and-sour flavor.

BUDGET TIP:

Skip the red wine and use extra water plus a splash more vinegar; it still gives you that classic sweet-and-sour *rotkohl* flavor for less. Make a big pot and freeze portions, because this side dish reheats beautifully and saves you from buying pricey sides later.

INGREDIENTS:

3 tbsp (39 g) bacon fat, (42 g) butter, or (45 ml) olive oil

2 cups (300 g) finely diced onions

1¾ lb (795 g) red cabbage, *shredded*

3 apples, *peeled, cored, and shredded or diced*

1 cup (240 ml) water

½ cup (120 ml) red wine *(optional)*

3 tbsp (45 ml) apple cider vinegar

2 tsp (8 g) granulated sugar

1 tsp (6 g) salt

½ tsp (1 g) freshly ground nutmeg

¼ tsp (0.5 g) ground cloves

¼ tsp (0.5 g) freshly ground black pepper

2 tbsp (30 ml) lemon juice

2 tbsp (16 g) cornstarch

INSTRUCTIONS:

1. In a large pot, heat the bacon fat over medium heat. Add the onions and sauté lightly.
2. Add the shredded cabbage and apples. Continue to sauté for several minutes.
3. Stir in the water, red wine, apple cider vinegar, sugar, salt, nutmeg, cloves, and pepper.
4. Bring to a simmer and cover. Simmer for about 30 to 60 minutes or until the cabbage is tender, adding more water if needed.
5. Add the lemon juice. Taste and season with more vinegar, sugar, salt, nutmeg, cloves, and/or pepper as needed.
6. Mix the cornstarch with a little bit of cold water and slowly stir just enough into the red cabbage to thicken the liquid. Serve.

TIPS:

For an extra quick version of this recipe, use canned or jarred red cabbage. Add shredded or grated apples. Simmer until the apples are cooked, about 10 minutes. Season and thicken with cornstarch as above.

The traditional recipe for red cabbage calls for cooking the cabbage until it's almost mush. If you prefer, you can slice the cabbage instead of shredding it and cook it for only about ½ an hour if you prefer a more textured cabbage dish.

Leftovers taste even better the next day.

This red cabbage freezes well.

PREP TIME:
40 min

COOK TIME:
35 min

TOTAL TIME:
1 hr 15 min

MAKES:
2–4 servings

Schupfnudeln

Potato Noodles

Schupfnudeln are a traditional German side dish that are so easy to make and are a great way to use up leftover potatoes.

Popular in the Baden-Württemberg area, but also found throughout Germany, these potato noodles are easily recognizable with their unusual shape. Because they almost look like little fingers, they are also known as *fingernudeln* or finger noodles. Definitely a fun and kid-friendly dinner choice!

BUDGET TIP:

Make a double batch and freeze the cooked *schupfnudeln* in a single layer. Then you can pull out a handful anytime and pan-fry them in butter for a quick, filling side dish without starting from scratch.

INGREDIENTS:

1½ lb (681 g) potatoes, *peeled and quartered*

2 tsp (12 g) salt

2 large egg yolks

4 tbsp (32 g) all-purpose flour, *plus more if needed*

2 tbsp (19 g) potato starch or (16 g) cornstarch

salt and freshly ground black pepper, *to taste*

freshly ground nutmeg, *to taste*

2 tbsp (28 g) butter

TIPS:

Starchy potatoes work best for this recipe, such as Russets or Yukon Golds.

If your potatoes aren't starchy enough, you may need to add a bit of extra flour to get the right consistency.

These noodles can also be enjoyed as a sweet treat served with vanilla sauce and sprinkled with cinnamon. You can even fry them up with apple slices for extra sweetness. Just be sure to omit the black pepper.

INSTRUCTIONS:

1. Cook the potatoes in boiling water until tender, about 20 minutes.
2. Drain the potatoes and let the steam escape to dry the potatoes (put the pot of potatoes back on the burner, briefly, to evaporate moisture, shaking the pot frequently so the potatoes don't burn).
3. Put a large pot of water on to boil. Add the salt, cover, and set it to simmer.
4. Mash the potatoes or put them through a ricer. Once cooled, add the egg yolks, flour, and potato starch. Mix together using your hands. Season with salt, pepper, and nutmeg.
5. Gently knead the dough, adding more flour as needed so that the dough doesn't stick to your hands.
6. Using floured hands, form half the dough into a log shape, about ½ an inch thick. Cut the log into 1-inch pieces. Roll each piece into a finger-sized noodle by rolling the dough between your hands. If the dough is too sticky, add a bit of flour. Each noodle should be thicker in the middle and tapered at the ends. Repeat with the remaining dough.
7. Drop half the noodles into the pot of simmering water and simmer until they float, about 5 minutes. Remove the noodles and drop them into a bowl of cold water. Once cool, drain. Repeat with remaining noodles.
8. Just before serving, melt the butter in a skillet over medium heat. Add the cooled, drained noodles and sauté for about 5 minutes, until golden brown and serve immediately.

PREP TIME:
2 min

COOK TIME:
8 min

TOTAL TIME:
10 min

MAKES:
4 servings

Schneller Rahmspinat

Quick Creamed Spinach

Are you in a hurry to make some traditional creamed spinach? Do you have frozen spinach in your freezer? Well then, you're blessed because you can enjoy this side dish in just 10 minutes!

BUDGET TIP:

Frozen spinach is usually far cheaper than fresh and already chopped, so nothing goes to waste. Skip the bacon bits and serve it with mashed potatoes and eggs to turn this into a full, low-cost German-style dinner.

INGREDIENTS:

3 10-oz (284-g) packages frozen chopped spinach

bacon bits *(optional)*

2–3 tbsp (16–24 g) cornstarch

2–3 tbsp (28–42 g) butter

salt and freshly ground black pepper, *to taste*

freshly ground nutmeg, *to taste*

INSTRUCTIONS:

1. Place the frozen spinach into a saucepan and add just enough water to cover the bottom of the pan, about half an inch deep.
2. Bring to a boil, then lower the heat to a simmer. Slowly stir as the spinach starts to thaw. Once thawed (it will only take a few minutes), let it simmer for several minutes. Add some bacon bits as the spinach simmers, if desired.
3. Dissolve the cornstarch in a bit of cold water. Slowly add just enough to the spinach to thicken the liquid to your liking. Stir in the butter until it melts.
4. Season with salt, pepper, nutmeg, and serve.

TIP:

For a really quick dinner, cook the spinach while you make mashed potatoes from a box of instant mashed potatoes (takes 5 minutes) and fry some eggs (takes 3 minutes).

Desserts

PREP TIME:
10 min

BAKE TIME:
50 min

TOTAL TIME:
1 hr

MAKES:
9 servings

Apfel-Puddingkuchen

Apple Pudding Cake

This apple pudding cake, aka *apfel-puddingkuchen*, tastes like a traditional apple bread pudding. It's an easy dessert recipe that's delicious served warm with ice cream and sprinkled with cinnamon.

Since it's prepared right in the baking dish, it's really super quick and easy.

BUDGET TIP:

This apple pudding cake uses inexpensive apples and pantry basics like flour, sugar, and milk. Serve it plain, with vanilla ice cream, or a simple dusting of powdered sugar instead of pricey toppings.

INGREDIENTS:

1 cup (130 g) all-purpose flour

1 cup (200 g) brown sugar

2 tsp (8 g) baking powder

½ tsp (3 g) salt

¼ tsp (0.75 g) cinnamon

4 apples, *peeled and sliced*

½ cup (120 ml) milk

1 tsp (5 ml) vanilla or almond extract

2–3 tsp (10-15 g) butter

2 cups (480 ml) boiling water

INSTRUCTIONS:

1. Preheat the oven to 400° F (205°C).
2. In a deep 9x9-inch pan, mix together the flour, brown sugar, baking powder, salt, and cinnamon.
3. Add the apple slices and mix until they are coated with the flour mixture.
4. Mix the milk with the vanilla and add it to the apple mixture.
5. Stir until everything has been moistened. Smooth out the top. Dot the butter on top.
6. Place the pan in the oven and carefully pour the boiling water over the top. DO NOT STIR. (Put a baking sheet on the rack under your pan. Sometimes it bubbles over when it's baking.)
7. Bake for 40 to 50 minutes or until the top is golden brown.
8. Let cool slightly before serving. Sprinkle extra cinnamon on top if desired.

TIPS:

Omit the cinnamon, if desired.

Sprinkle slivered almonds on top before baking.

Serve with whipped cream, vanilla ice cream, or vanilla sauce.

PREP TIME:
10 min

RISE TIME:
2 hrs

BAKE TIME:
20 min

TOTAL TIME:
2 hrs 30 min

MAKES:
16 slices

Butterkuchen

Butter Cake

Butterkuchen is a favorite that's often served for afternoon *kaffeeklatsch*. I also like it since it's super easy to make. For this version, I use my bread machine. You can use this method for most of your yeast cakes to make prepping, kneading, and proofing the dough easier. Then finish the rest of the recipe by hand and bake. It's an easy and convenient method to master.

However, if you don't have a bread machine or you want to make the dough by hand, simply follow your usual yeast baking recipe, but use the ingredients I've listed here.

BUDGET TIP:

Butterkuchen feels like a bakery treat, but it's made from simple yeast dough ingredients you probably already have. Skip the heavy cream topping if you want to save money, and bake it in a 9x13-inch pan to get lots of slices for the cost of one small dessert.

INGREDIENTS: FOR THE YEAST DOUGH:

2 tsp (7 g) instant yeast

¼ cup (50 g) granulated sugar

2¼ cups (293 g) all-purpose flour

1 tsp (6 g) salt

⅞ cup (210 ml) lukewarm milk

1 egg yolk

1 tbsp (14 g) unsalted butter, *softened*

FOR THE TOPPING:

3 tbsp (42 g) unsalted butter, *cold*

½ cup (50 g) sliced almonds

⅓ cup (67 g) granulated sugar

cinnamon *(optional)*

⅓ cup (80 ml) heavy *(whipping)* cream *(optional)*

INSTRUCTIONS:

1. Put all the yeast dough ingredients into the bread machine pan. Use the dough setting and start. This usually takes about 1½ hours.
2. Grease a rimmed 9x13-inch baking sheet or two 9-inch springform pans.
3. Once the dough cycle is finished, pat the dough onto the baking sheet with oiled hands.
4. Dimple the surface with your finger. Push bits of the butter into the indentations. Sprinkle with the almonds, sugar, and cinnamon.
5. Cover with a towel and let stand in a warm, draft-free place for 20 to 30 minutes. Meanwhile, preheat the oven to 390°F (199°C).
6. Bake for 20 to 25 minutes or until golden. If using heavy cream, pour it over the cake as soon as you take it out of the oven. Let cool slightly. Best served warm from the oven.

TIP:

For the cake pictured, I made it in two springform pans, sprinkling cinnamon over one (top row) and pouring heavy cream over the other. Two cakes made in the time of one!

PREP TIME:
20 min

BAKE TIME:
30 min

TOTAL TIME:
50 min

MAKES:
1 strudel + enough dough for 2 more strudels

Einfacher Apfelstrudel

Easy Apple Strudel

This recipe was given to me, and often made for me, by my dear friend, Melania Orasch. Austrian in origin, this strudel is so wonderfully flaky! The ingredients are usually already in my pantry, and there are always a couple of extra apples in the crisper, so it's quick to put together.

Although this is not a traditional German recipe, it's been a hit with our family. Melania often fills hers with apples, cheese, walnuts, or dried fruits. This recipe is the apple one, which is my favorite!

BUDGET TIP:

This recipe is a money-saver because the dough makes enough for three strudels. Bake one now, then wrap and freeze the extra dough portions so you can make two more desserts later with just a few apples and pantry basics.

INGREDIENTS:
FOR THE DOUGH:

3 cups (390 g) all-purpose flour

2 tsp (12 g) salt

1 cup (227 g) lard

2 large eggs, *beaten*

¾ cup (180 ml) ginger ale

FOR THE FILLING:

1 lb (454 g) apples, *peeled and diced*

small handful of raisins

2 tbsp (26 g) granulated sugar

cinnamon

powdered sugar, *for dusting*

INSTRUCTIONS:

1. Preheat the oven to 350°F (180°C). Line a baking sheet with parchment paper and set aside.
2. Mix the flour and salt together. Cut in the lard. Add the beaten eggs and ginger ale. Gather together and knead slightly. Form into a ball. Divide into three parts. Wrap two parts with plastic wrap and refrigerate or put in the freezer for longer storage.
3. On a lightly floured counter, roll out the remaining part as thinly as possible into a rectangle, around 12x16 inches.
4. Spread the apples on the dough, keeping 2 inches from the long edge and 1 inch from the short ends. Sprinkle the raisins and sugar over the apples and dust with cinnamon. Fold the edges over and roll up the strudel lengthwise. Slash the top diagonally about 3 times.
5. Place the strudel seam side down on the baking sheet.
6. Bake for 30 minutes, or until golden brown.
7. Let cool before sprinkling with powdered sugar and serve.

PREP TIME:
15 min

COOK TIME:
15 min

TOTAL TIME:
30 min

MAKES:
4 servings

Kaiserschmarrn

Torn Pancakes

These torn pancakes are a fun and shareable dessert (or sweet main dish). They are dusted with powdered sugar and often served with applesauce or warm plum compote.

BUDGET TIP:

Kaiserschmarrn is a wonderful cheap dessert dinner because it's mostly eggs, flour, and milk. Skip the raisins if you don't have them, and serve it with applesauce instead of fresh fruit for a classic topping that costs a lot less.

INGREDIENTS:

4 large eggs, *separated*

¾ cup (98 g) all-purpose flour

½ cup (120 ml) milk

1 pinch salt

1 tsp (4 g) baking powder

2 tbsp (26 g) granulated sugar

4 oz (113 g) raisins

4 tbsp (56 g) butter, *divided*

powdered sugar, *for dusting*

INSTRUCTIONS:

1. In a large bowl, add the egg yolks, flour, milk, salt, baking powder, and sugar, and mix well. Let the batter stand for 10 minutes.
2. Meanwhile, beat the egg whites until stiff peaks form.
3. Gently fold the stiff egg whites into the batter.
4. Gently fold in the raisins.
5. In a large frying pan, melt 2 tablespoons (28 grams) of the butter over medium heat. Pour the pancake batter into the hot pan and fry until golden brown on the bottom.
6. Flip the pancake, adding the remaining butter, and continue to cook the other side until browned.
7. Using two forks, tear the pancake into bite-size pieces and continue cooking briefly.
8. Serve, dusted with powdered sugar.

TIPS:

You can omit the raisins. Or, you can soak the raisins in rum first, then add the drained raisins to the batter.

Add 1 teaspoon (4 grams) vanilla sugar or ½ teaspoon (2.5 milliliters) vanilla extract, if desired.

PREP TIME:
20 min

DEEP FRY TIME:
3 min

TOTAL TIME:
23 min

MAKES:
60 cookies

Räderkuchen

Wheel Cakes

Similar to *mutzenmandeln*, *Kameruner*, *durchzoggene*, and other types of *schmalzgebäck* (deep-fried pastries), my *mutti's räderkuchen* were among her favorite cookies to make when unexpected company dropped by. They were so quick to prepare with ingredients that were always in her pantry.

Deep-fried and covered in sugar or a cinnamon-sugar mix, *räderkuchen* taste like little doughnuts and are absolutely *WUNDERBAR!*

BUDGET TIP:

Skip buying pre-made treats and make these instead. *Räderkuchen* use simple pantry basics, so you can make a big batch (about 60). Roll them in plain sugar if you want to keep it extra affordable.

INGREDIENTS:

2 tbsp (28 g) butter, *room temperature*

3 tbsp (39 g) granulated sugar

3 large eggs

3 tbsp (45 ml) milk

2 cups (260 g) all-purpose flour

2 tsp (8 g) baking powder

lard, *for frying*

cinnamon sugar, *to garnish*

TIPS:

To make cinnamon sugar, whisk together ½ cup (100 grams) granulated sugar with 1–2 tablespoons (9 to 18 grams) ground cinnamon. Store in a glass jar or container with a tight-fitting lid.

You can also roll the cookies in plain granulated sugar or powdered sugar.

INSTRUCTIONS:

1. Cover a large plate with paper towels and set aside.
2. Put the butter, sugar, eggs, milk, flour, and baking powder into a large mixing bowl and mix together to make a dough.
3. Form the dough into a ball, adding a little extra flour if the dough is too sticky. Alternatively, chill the dough in the fridge to let it firm up.
4. Roll half the dough into a ⅜-inch thick rectangle on a lightly floured counter.
5. Cut the dough into 1-inch wide strips. Cut each strip into 3-inch long pieces. About ½-inch from one end of each piece, cut a 1-inch long slot. Pull the long end of the strip through the slot. Repeat with the remaining dough. Any excess dough can be rerolled.

6. Heat the lard in a deep pot to about 360°F (182°C). If you don't have a thermometer, insert the dry end of a wooden spoon. If bubbles form around it, the oil is ready.
7. Carefully place several cookies into the hot fat. After a minute or so, when the edges are golden brown, flip and fry the other side till golden.
8. Use a spider or slotted spoon to remove the cookies, then place them on the paper towel-lined plate to drain.
9. While they are still hot, roll the cookies in the cinnamon sugar and place them on a wire rack to cool. Repeat with the remaining cookies. Enjoy fresh!

Pantry Staples List

Baking & Dry Goods:

- ○ All-purpose flour
- ○ Bread flour
- ○ Potato starch or cornstarch
- ○ Baking powder
- ○ Baking soda
- ○ CREAM OF WHEAT *(not instant)*
- ○ Granulated sugar
- ○ Powdered sugar
- ○ Vanilla sugar *(optional)*
- ○ Cinnamon
- ○ Raisins *(optional)*
- ○ Egg noodles

Potatoes & Bread Basics:

- ○ Potatoes *(Yukon Gold or any starchy potatoes)*
- ○ Instant mashed potato flakes *(optional, for thickening soups)*
- ○ Bread *(for Arme Ritter, page 50; best with day-old bread)*

Broth & Soup Helpers:

- ○ Bouillon cubes to make broth *(vegetable and chicken)*

Oils & Fats:

- ○ Olive oil
- ○ Neutral oil for frying *(like canola)*
- ○ Butter
- ○ Bacon fat *(optional)*
- ○ Lard *(for frying, optional)*

Dairy:

- ○ Milk
- ○ Heavy cream *(optional)*
- ○ Sour cream *(optional topping)*

Eggs & Meat:

- ○ Eggs
- ○ Rotisserie chicken *(or leftover cooked chicken)*
- ○ Boneless skinless chicken thighs *(optional alternative)*
- ○ Canned corned beef
- ○ Bacon *(optional)*

Canned & Jarred Staples:

- ○ Canned sliced red beets
- ○ Jarred or canned red cabbage *(optional shortcut)*
- ○ Pickles
- ○ Ginger ale *(for Easy Apple Strudel dough, page 90)*

Vegetables & Fruit:

- ○ Onions
- ○ Garlic *(optional)*
- ○ Carrots
- ○ Celery
- ○ Leeks
- ○ Cabbage *(green or savoy)*
- ○ Red cabbage
- ○ Mushrooms *(white or cremini)*
- ○ Frozen mixed vegetables
- ○ Frozen peas *(optional)*
- ○ Apples
- ○ Lemons *(or lemon juice)*
- ○ Fresh parsley *(optional garnish)*

Seasoning & Flavor Boosters:

- ○ Salt
- ○ Black pepper
- ○ Nutmeg
- ○ Ground cloves
- ○ MAGGI liquid seasoning *(optional but very Oma-approved)*
- ○ VEGETA seasoning *(optional, also Oma-approved)*
- ○ Bay leaves

WANT MORE FROM OMA?

Shop Oma's cookbook catalog:

shop.justlikeoma.com

Get new recipes and new releases by email:

quick-german-recipes.com/newsletter

I've enjoyed sharing my recipes with you and would love to hear from you with any comments. Pop over to my private facebook.com/groups/kaffeeklatschers group and say, "Hallo!"

"The secret ingredient is always love!"

-Oma Gerhild

www.ingramcontent.com/pod-product-compliance
Lightning Source LLC
LaVergne TN
LVHW010836120826
845149LV00017B/1475

* 9 7 8 1 9 9 7 8 8 6 0 5 1 *